Everyday Survival English

Karl Nordvall

Compass Publishing

Everyday Survival English

Karl Nordvall

© 2005 Compass Publishing Inc.

Acquisitions Editor: Casey Malarcher
Cover/Interior Design: Design Plus
Illustrations: Hieram Weintraub

email: info@compasspub.com
http://www.compasspub.com

ISBN: 978-1-932222-47-0

13
11

Preface

Everyday Survival English is a ready resource that provides basic vocabulary and structures useful for talking with others in a variety of situations in English. Through the 72 situations presented in the book, readers will encounter a wide range of high frequency phrases and sentences that are directly applicable to many situations they might encounter while living or traveling in an English speaking country.

A key feature of this book is the comic format used to guide readers through various aspects of the situations within each unit. The pictures not only provide visual clues and labels to aid in comprehension, but also help readers in guessing the meaning of unfamiliar English words through the context of the picture and situation. Additionally, the audio CD recording of the text is useful for familiarizing English language learners with the sound of words and phrases as spoken by native speakers. The audio recording can be used for both listening and pronunciation practice.

The following characters appear throughout *Everyday Survival English* as guides along each reader's English journey.

Kim   John   Julia

Peter   Mary   Carlos

Contents

UNIT 1 Introductions

Words and Phrases to Learn

- *call*: to use as my name
- *nothing special*: just the usual
- *come have*: to come over and have (sth)
- *see you then*: to see you at that time

Key Expressions

[1] Austin is my hometown.
 = I grew up in Austin.
[2] What are your plans this evening? = What are you up to this evening?

Mary sees her new neighbor.

They walk toward each other....

....and shake hands.

Mary asks where Kim is from.

They talk.

Mary asks about Kim's evening schedule.

Mary invites Kim to her house.

They say good-bye.

UNIT 2 — The Visit

Words and Phrases to Learn
- *greet*: to say hello
- *look around*: to walk around and look
- *offer*: to ask if (sb) wants (sth)
- *our pleasure*: we're glad you could come

Key Expressions
1. Would you like...
   = Can I get you...
2. Orange juice sounds good.
   = I'd like some orange juice.

Kim arrives at John and Mary's house.

Mary hangs up Kim's jacket.

Mary introduces John to Kim.

John and Kim greet each other and shake hands.

They go into another room.

Kim looks around the house.

Mary offers Kim a drink....

....and tells her the choices.

UNIT **3** Occupations

Words and Phrases to Learn
- *describe*: to tell about
- *offer a seat*: to ask if (sb) wants to sit
- *accounts*: the dept. that manages bank accounts
- *part-time*: around 20 hours or less a week

Key Expressions
1 I'm looking for a new job. = I'm trying to find a new position.
2 What do you do? = What kind of job do you have?

John offers Kim a seat.

John and Kim sit down.

John asks Kim about her job.

John asks if Kim enjoys her work.

John tells Kim about his work.

Mary brings the drinks....

.....and sits down.

Mary describes her job at the bank.

Words and Phrases to Learn
- *pet*: to touch continuously
- *sophomore*: a 2ⁿᵈ year student
- *MBA*: Master's degree in Business Administration
- *small world*: how surprising (sb) is in same place

Key Expressions
1. What was your major in college?
   = What did you study at university?
2. Where did you go to school? = What university did you study at?

Mary and John's dog comes in.

Kim pets Sam.

Kim asks Mary's major.

Kim talks about her education.

The dog walks over to John....

....and John picks him up.

Kim puts down her drink.

Mary shows Kim to the bathroom.

UNIT 5 Family

Words and Phrases to Learn
- *pass away*: to die
- *express*: to show
- *sympathy*: care
- *only child*: (sb) having no brothers or sisters

Key Expressions
1. How many people are in your family? = Do you have any brothers or sisters?
2. Where's your hometown? = Where are you from?

That's a nice wedding picture. When did you get married?

Three years ago.

Kim comes back and looks at a picture.

Are those your parents, Mary?

Yes. And my brother is standing next to them.

picture frame

Kim asks about the people in the picture.

The woman in the purple dress is John's mother.

My dad passed away when I was in college.

Mary and John talk about their family.

I'm sorry to hear that.

Thank you. We miss him a lot.

Kim expresses her sympathy...

1 How many people are in your family, Kim?

I have three brothers and one sister.

...and sits down again.

That's really big! Are you the oldest?

No, I'm the second oldest.

Mary asks Kim about her place in the family.

2 Where's your hometown, John?

I'm from Seattle. My mom still lives there.

Kim turns to John...

Do you have any brothers or sisters?

No. I'm an only child.

...and asks about his family.

UNIT 6 Saying Good-bye

Mary checks on her guest.

Kim notices the time.

They stand up....

....and walk to the door.

Mary goes to the kitchen.

Kim puts on her jacket.

Mary gives the jam to Kim.

Kim walks out the door.

UNIT 1 Women's Clothing

The saleswoman greets Julia.

The saleswoman points to the skirts.

Julia asks for a beige skirt.

The saleswoman looks through the skirts.

The saleswoman takes a skirt off the rack.

Julia points to the display.

The saleswoman finds Julia a light blue blouse.

Julia takes the blouse from the saleswoman.

Words and Phrases to Learn
- *a pair of*: two; a set of
- *fit*: match (sb's) size
- *counter*: a long table for showing goods
- *tight*: too small

Key Expressions
1. I'll take them.
   = I would like (to buy) them.
2. I'm not sure.
   = I don't really know.

curtain

Julia tries on the blouse and skirt.

Julia decides to buy the skirt and blouse.

The saleswoman puts the clothes on the counter.

The saleswoman shows Julia some sandals.

Julia tells her shoe size.

The saleswoman brings two boxes.

mirror

Julia puts on a shoe.

Julia is happy with the other sandals.

UNIT 3 Men's Clothing

Peter goes into a men's clothing store.

The salesman and Peter stand by the jeans display.

Peter tells the salesman his size.

He chooses a pair of jeans.

The salesman tells Peter about a sale.

Peter asks about the material.

Peter rubs the material.

The salesman hands Peter a large T-shirt.

15

Words and Phrases to Learn
- *charge*: payment by credit card
- *try on*: to put on and check for size
- *swipe*: to move (sth) quickly through a reading machine
- *receipt*: a list showing the prices of items and the total

Key Expressions
1. Your total is $65.
   = That comes to $65.
2. Bring it back with your receipt.
   = Return it with your receipt.

The salesman and Peter go to the counter.

The salesman takes Peter's payment.

The salesman swipes Peter's credit card.

Peter signs the receipt.

Peter takes his receipt and credit card.

The salesman puts Peter's clothes in a bag.

The salesman gives Peter the bag.

Peter leaves the store.

UNIT 5 Electronics

Words and Phrases to Learn
- *salesclerk*: (sb) working in a store
- *warranty*: a promise to fix a product
- *cheaper*: less expensive
- *features*: special things on/about

Key Expressions
1. What kind would you like? = What kind are you looking for?
2. The camera comes with a free bag. = You get a free bag when you buy the camera.

Kim enters an electronics shop.

The salesclerk shows Kim some cameras.

The salesclerk picks up a camera.

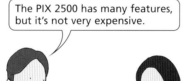

Kim looks at the camera.

Kim asks about the camera.

Kim decides to buy the camera.

The salesclerk gives Kim a camera bag.

Kim pays for the camera.

Words and Phrases to Learn
- *scratched*: damaged by a mark
- *cash register*: a machine that adds purchases and holds money
- *exchange*: to change for a new or different one
- *refund*: the money a customer gets for returning an item

Key Expressions
1. I'm sorry for the trouble. = I apologize for the inconvenience.
2. No problem. = That's OK.

Hi. May I help you?

Yes, I want to return a camera.

Kim goes back to the electronics shop.

I bought this here yesterday, but the lens was already scratched.

May I look at it, please?

Kim takes her camera out of her bag.

I see it. I'm sorry about that, ma'am.

The salesclerk looks at the camera.

Would you like to exchange the camera or get a refund?

I'd like to exchange it, please.

Kim asks for another camera.

Do you have the receipt?

Yes, here you are.

receipt

Kim gives the salesclerk her receipt.

Would you like the same camera, or another kind?

I'd like the same model, please.

The salesclerk puts the receipt in the cash register.

Here you are. Does this one look good?

Yes. This one looks fine.

Kim looks at her new camera.

1 I'm sorry for the trouble.

2 No problem. Have a nice day.

You too, ma'am.

Kim goes to the door.

UNIT 1 — At a Fast Food Restaurant

Words and Phrases to Learn
- *place (an order)*: to make or give (an order)
- *meal*: kinds of food served together
- *packets*: small packages
- *trash*: garbage

Key Expressions
1. Is that for here or to go? = To eat in or take out?
2. I'm finished. = I'm done.

John and Mary talk about what to order.

John places his order at the counter.

Mary asks for a burger without pickles.

The cashier asks if it's for take-out.

The cashier gives them their food.

The cashier puts some more ketchup packets on the tray.

Mary gets some straws from the dispenser.

After lunch, John throws away the trash.

UNIT 2 At the Movies

Words and Phrases to Learn
- *snacks*: food eaten between meals
- *pass*: to hand; to give
- *usher*: (sb) working in a theater who takes tickets and tells people where to go
- *stub*: a part torn from a ticket

Key Expressions
1. I heard that movie is good.
   = That movie got good reviews.
2. It is on your left. = It is to the left.

Carlos and Julia walk into the movie theater.

Carlos chooses tickets for the 8:00 show.

The cashier passes the tickets through the window.

They get some snacks.

Carlos gives their tickets to the usher.

The usher takes the tickets and gives back the stubs.

They choose a place to sit.

Carlos and Julia watch the movie.

UNIT 3 Ordering Pizza

Words and Phrases to Learn
- *address*: the number for a house
- *delivery person*: (sb) who brings things to one's house
- *change*: extra money over the total
- *tip*: money given for good service

Key Expressions
1. Anything else?
   = Will that be all?
2. Keep the change. = I don't need any change back.

John puts the video in the VCR.

Peter dials the number of the pizza restaurant.

Peter places his order.

The Pizza Patrol worker writes down Peter's order.

Peter gives his address to the Pizza Patrol worker.

The Pizza Patrol worker tells Peter the price.

The delivery person comes with the pizza.

Peter gives the delivery person $2 as a tip.

Words and Phrases to Learn
- *sure*: really
- *grocery bag*: a bag from a supermarket
- *take out (the trash)*: to carry outside
- *garbage bag*: a bag for waste

Key Expressions
1. Let me get the door for you.
   = I will open the door for you.
2. Where should I put these?
   = Where do these go?

Hi, Mrs. Price. Can I help you?

Hi, Peter. That would be great. Thank you!

Peter offers to carry grocery bags for Mrs. Price.

You sure got a lot of food!

Well, my grandchildren are visiting tomorrow.

Peter carries the bags to the apartment.

I see. That will be nice.

Yes. ¹Let me get the door for you.

Mrs. Price opens her apartment door.

²Where should I put these?

Please put them on the kitchen counter.

Mrs. Price tells Peter where to put the bags.

Right here?

Yes. That's fine. Thank you so much!

Peter puts the bags on the kitchen counter.

Is there anything else I can do for you?

Peter asks if he can still help.

Would you mind taking out my trash?

cupboards

Mrs. Price points to the garbage can.

Of course not.

I'm so glad to have a neighbor like you, Peter!

Peter picks up the garbage bag.

UNIT 5 At a Coffee Shop

Words and Phrases to Learn
- *decaffeinated*: without caffeine
- *pick-up counter*: the counter where customers take things
- *pour*: to make (sth) like water come out
- *stir*: to move around with a spoon

Key Expressions
1. Can you get (sth) for me?
   = Would you bring me (sth)?
2. They sit down by the window.
   = They take a seat by the window.

Hi, welcome to Moonbucks. How can I help you?

I'll have a large coffee.

Mary and Kim go to the coffee shop counter.

Regular or decaf, ma'am?

Decaf, please.

Mary asks for decaffeinated coffee.

I'd like a low-fat cappuccino, please.

OK. Would you like anything else?

No, thanks.

Kim places her order.

That will be $6.50, please. You can get your drinks over there.

The cashier points to the pick-up counter.

Thanks.

A large decaf and a low-fat cappuccino. Here you go.

Mary gets their coffee.

1Can you get some cream and sugar for me?

Sure.

Kim picks up some sugar packets and cream for Mary.

Have you seen the Renoir exhibit at the art museum?

Yes. I went last weekend. It was wonderful!

2They sit down at a table by the window.

Peter wants to see it, too. You should go together.

Great idea. I'll give him a call.

Mary pours some cream into her coffee and stirs it.

Words and Phrases to Learn

- *request*: to ask for
- *works*: things made by an artist
- *amazing*: surprising and great
- *sculpture*: art like a statue

Key Expressions

1. Let's go Dutch.
   = Let's split the bill.
2. You can't take pictures here.
   = Pictures are not allowed here.

Peter requests two tickets.

Kim reaches for her purse.

They agree to share the cost of the tickets.

The ticket seller points to the schedule.

Kim and Peter go on the tour.

Kim tries to take a picture.

Peter asks a question about the sculpture.

Kim and Peter talk about what they have seen.

UNIT 1 — Taking a Taxi

Words and Phrases to Learn
- *cab*: a taxi
- *hail*: to call (a taxi)
- *turn on*: to start
- *chat*: to talk

Key Expressions
1. After you. = Ladies' first.
2. That'll be... = The total comes to...

Peter and Kim decide to take a taxi.

Peter hails a taxi.

Peter opens the door for Kim.

Peter gives the driver directions.

The taxi driver turns on the meter.

They chat with the driver.

The taxi stops in front of the concert hall.

Peter pays the fare.

UNIT 2 — In the Library

Words and Phrases to Learn
- *call number*: the identifying library number of a book
- *recommend*: to suggest
- *jacket*: a removable cover
- *century*: a period of a hundred years

Key Expressions
1. What's it about? = What's the story?
2. When should we return these? = When do these have to be back?

Julia and Carlos walk into the library.

Julia searches for a book.

Julia writes down the book's call number.

They walk down the aisle.

Julia pulls the book off the shelf.

Julia reads the jacket of the book...

...and recommends the book to Carlos.

They check out their books.

UNIT 3 Taking a Bus

Words and Phrases to Learn
- *mall*: a big shopping center
- *get on*: to enter a car / bus / train
- *fare*: money (sb) must pay to ride (sth)
- *ring*: to signal

Key Expressions
[1] You have to take bus number 400. = The 400 goes that way.
[2] You're so kind!
   = That's very nice of you!

Kim asks a person about the bus schedule.

The person tells Kim which bus to take.

Kim sits down on the bench.

Kim gets on the bus.

The bus driver tells Kim the fare.

Kim asks how far the mall is.

Kim offers her seat to another person.

Kim rings for her stop.

Words and Phrases to Learn
- *unscrew*: to turn and open
- *insert*: to put in
- *squeeze*: to press together
- *unleaded*: gas with less lead in it

Key Expressions
1 up ahead = coming up
2 It saves money.
   = It's cheaper that way.

Julia points down the road.

They pull into the self-serve lane at the station.

Julia gets out of the car.

Julia unscrews the gas cap.

Julia takes the nozzle off the pump and lifts the lever.

Julia inserts the nozzle and squeezes the handle.

Carlos puts a pack of gum on the counter.

Carlos pays the cashier.

UNIT 5 Asking for Directions

Julia and Carlos are lost.

Julia asks for directions.

The man cannot help them.

Julia asks another person.

The woman points down the road.

The woman gives them more directions.

Julia confirms the directions.

Julia thanks the woman for her help.

Words and Phrases to Learn
- *connect*: to hook up; to access
- *log on*: to enter a website
- *be open*: to be available
- *service*: computer use

Key Expressions
1. What are your rates?
   = How much do you charge per hour?
2. I'll get your coffee.
   = I'll just go bring you your coffee.

Good afternoon!

Hi. I'd like to use the Internet.

Kim walks into an Internet cafe.

OK. Will you be playing online games, chatting or just using email?

I just want to send email.[1] What are your rates?

The man asks what kind of service Kim will be using.

It's $1 for the first 10 minutes. After that, it's 5 cents per minute. You also get a free cup of coffee.

The man describes the rates.

Station number 9 is open.

Alright. Sounds good.

Kim follows the man to a computer.

Here you are.[2] I'll get your coffee.

Thank you.

Kim sits down at the station.

Excuse me. How do I connect to the Internet?

Kim turns to the person next to her for help.

Just click on the icon at the bottom of the screen.

Thanks!

The woman tells Kim how to start.

Wow! I have a lot of new messages!

FLASHMAIL

Kim logs on to her email account.

CHAPTER 5. RESTAURANT

UNIT 1 — Arriving at the Restaurant

Words and Phrases to Learn
- *reservation*: a request to keep (sth) for a customer
- *host*: a restaurant employee who shows people where to sit
- *satisfied*: OK; happy with (sth)
- *shortly*: soon

Key Expressions
1. Follow me.
   = This way, please.
2. Will this be all right?
   = Is this table OK?

John checks in with the host.

The host checks the reservation list.

The couple follows the host to the table.

The host asks the couple if they are satisfied.

John asks for a different table.

The host takes them to another table.

The host gives them menus and then tells them about the specials.

The host leaves.

Words and Phrases to Learn
- *delicious*: very tasty
- *appetizer*: a small dish served before a meal
- *honey*: a term used to refer to (sb) you love
- *decide*: to finally choose one thing

Key Expressions
1. Can I get you anything to drink?
   = What would you like to drink?
2. I'll be right back with (sth). = I will go and get (sth) for you.

The couple looks at their menus.

The waiter arrives and introduces himself.

The waiter asks if they would like anything to drink.

John orders a beer.

Mary orders her drink.

The waiter asks if they would like an appetizer.

The couple looks at the menu and decides.

The waiter leaves.

UNIT 3 The Waiter Returns

Words and Phrases to Learn
- *dressing*: sauce served on salad
- *side dishes*: foods served along with the main dish
- *medium rare*: (sth) cooked between rare and medium
- *dish*: one kind of food

Key Expressions
1 Are you ready to order?
  = Have you decided what you'd like?
2 How would you like that?
  = How should that be cooked?

Here you are.

The waiter brings the drinks and the appetizer.

[1]Are you ready to order?

Yes, I'll have the New York steak.

The couple is ready to order.

[2]How would you like that?

Medium rare, please.

The waiter asks Mary how she would like her steak cooked.

OK. That comes with a potato, soup, or salad.

I'll have a salad, please.

The waiter tells Mary about the side dishes.

We have French, Ranch, Thousand Island, and Italian dressing.

Ranch, please.

The waiter asks her what kind of dressing she wants.

What's in your seafood spaghetti?

Crab, squid, and clams.

John asks about the dish he wants.

OK, I'll have that with a cup of onion soup.

John tells the waiter what side dish he wants.

Will that be all?

Yes, thanks.

OK, call me if you need anything else.

The waiter takes the menus.

Words and Phrases to Learn
- *pasta*: noodles or food made from flour paste
- *parmesan cheese*: a kind of cheese usually served over spaghetti
- *plate*: dish that food is served on
- *dishes*: plates, cups, bowls, etc.

Key Expressions
1 It's perfect.
  = It's just the way I like it.
2 I'll take these plates away.
  = Let me get these plates out of the way.

The waiter brings the food.

Here you are. New York steak ... and for you, sir, seafood spaghetti.

He puts the food on the table.

Is your steak all right?

The waiter asks Mary about her steak.

Yes, [1] it's perfect.

Mary cuts into her steak.

Would you like some parmesan on your pasta?

Sure!

bowl

The waiter offers John some parmesan cheese.

[2]I'll take these plates away.

The waiter takes the appetizer dishes from the table.

No, thanks.

Can I get you anything else?

The waiter asks if they need anything else.

OK, then. Enjoy your meal.

The waiter tells them to have a nice meal.

UNIT **5** A Lovely Meal

Words and Phrases to Learn
- *dessert*: a sweet food served after a meal
- *decline*: to say no
- *the rest*: the extra; the remaining part(s)
- *excellent*: unusually good

Key Expressions
1 Could I take the rest home?
  = Can I get a take-home box for the rest?
2 I'll wrap it up for you.
  = I'll put it in a box for you.

John and Mary enjoy their meal.

The waiter comes back to check on the couple.

The waiter asks about dessert.

Mary declines.

Mary asks for a take-home box.

The waiter takes the plates from the table.

John and Mary are very satisfied with the meal.

The waiter comes back with the take-home box.

Words and Phrases to Learn

- *bill*: a list of charges for service, foods, etc.
- *right*: directly; immediately
- *sign*: to write one's name
- *get up*: to stand

Key Expressions

1. Could we have the bill?
   = Can we get the check?
2. I'll pay the tip.
   = Let me get the tip.

[1] Could we have the bill, please?

John asks for the bill.

Here's your bill.

bill

The waiter brings the bill.

Thank you. I'll be right back.

John gives his credit card to the waiter.

Honey, [2] I'll pay the tip. Five dollars should be fine.

Mary offers to get the tip.

Your card and receipt, sir.

The waiter returns with the credit card and receipt.

John signs the receipt.

Here's your copy of the receipt.

The waiter gives John a copy of the signed receipt.

Thank you and come again!

Thanks. Good-bye.

The waiter thanks the couple as they get up to leave.

UNIT 1 — At the Post Office

Words and Phrases to Learn
- *surface mail*: not airmail; mail sent by boat or truck
- *priority mail*: express mail
- *document*: an important paper
- *business day*: workday; weekday

Key Expressions
1. How long would it take by priority mail? = How many days does priority mail take?
2. How much will that be in total? = How much do I owe?

What can I do for you today?

I'd like to send this package to London.

Peter puts a package on the counter.

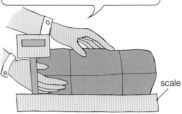

If you send it by surface mail, it will cost $8. It should get there in four to six weeks.

scale

The postal worker puts the package on a scale.

What about air mail?

That would be $25. It would arrive in 10 days.

I'll do that.

Peter chooses to send it by air.

You can get insurance for $3.

That's a good idea. I'd also like to mail these papers to New York.

Peter takes out some documents.

Do you want to use regular mail, priority mail, or express mail?

Three business days.

1 How long would it take by priority mail?

The postal worker and Peter discuss mailing options.

I'll use priority mail, please.

OK. Please put your papers in this envelope and write the address.

The postal worker hands a priority mail envelope to Peter.

2 How much will this be in total?

That's $35, please.

Peter writes the address on the envelope.

Here you are.

Thank you. Have a nice day.

Thanks, you too.

Peter pays the postal worker.

Words and Phrases to Learn
- *teller*: (sb) serving customers at a bank
- *denomination*: the value of the money, e.g. $10 bill
- *traveler's cheques*: cheques guaranteed by the bank
- *fee*: money paid for a service

Key Expressions
1. What size bills...
   = What denomination bills...
2. How many and what denomination would you like?
   = How would you like your traveler's cheques?

Good afternoon! How can I help you?

Hi, I'd like to exchange US dollars for British pounds.

Kim comes up to the counter at the bank.

How much would you like to exchange?

Two hundred dollars, please.

Kim takes the money out of her purse.

May I see your passport?

Yes, here you are.

passport

Kim gives her passport and money to the teller.

All right. That's 125 pounds.[1] What size bills would you like?

Five twenties, two tens, and a five, please.

The teller changes the money.

I would also like some traveler's cheques.

[2] How many and what denomination would you like?

I'd like six 50 dollar cheques, please.

bill

Kim counts the British money.

With the fee, your total is $307.

Here you are.

Kim pays for the traveler's cheques.

Please sign each cheque now.

Kim signs the traveler's cheques.

You're welcome. Have a great trip.

Thanks for your help.

Kim puts the cash and cheques into her purse.

UNIT **3** Dropping Off Dry Cleaning

Words and Phrases to Learn
- *fill out*: to write in the necessary information
- *claim ticket*: a receipt to get (sth)
- *as good as new*: very clean and tidy
- *garment*: a piece of clothing

Key Expressions
1. That won't be a problem.
   = That stain will come out.
2. When can I pick it up?
   = When will it be ready?

Mary puts some clothes on the counter.

Mary takes her blouse out of the bag.

The dry cleaner looks at the blouse.

Mary fills out the tag.

The dry cleaner tears off the claim ticket and gives it to Mary.

The next day, Mary shows her claim ticket to the dry cleaner.

The dry cleaner gives back Mary's garment.

Mary looks at her blouse.

Words and Phrases to Learn
- *doubles*: an extra copy of every picture
- *print*: a photo
- *develop*: to get photos made from film
- *exposure*: picture

Key Expressions
1 Standard size, please.
  = 3 (inch) by 5 (inch), please.
2 Can I get your name, please?
  = What is your name, please?

Carlos puts his roll of film on the counter.

The shopkeeper puts the roll of film in an envelope.

The shopkeeper writes the information on the envelope.

Carlos spells his last name for the shopkeeper.

The shopkeeper gives Carlos his claim ticket.

Carlos points to the film rack.

The shopkeeper gives Carlos some choices.

The shopkeeper hands the film to Carlos.

UNIT 5 At the Video Store

Julia and Carlos walk into a video store.

Carlos asks the cashier about the movie.

The cashier looks for the movie's name in the computer.

Carlos and Julia head to the new release section.

Julia picks up a video and reads the back cover.

Julia gives her membership card to the clerk.

The clerk scans Julia's card.

Julia gets the video.

UNIT Getting a Haircut

Words and Phrases to Learn
- *trim*: to cut a little bit
- *barber*: (sb) who cuts men's hair
- *sideburn*: hair that grows on the cheek in front of the ear (on men)
- *trimmer*: an electric shaver for long hair

Key Expressions
1. How can I help you?
   = What can I do for you?
2. Please have a seat.
   = Please sit down.

John hangs up his jacket.

The barber points to an empty barber chair.

The barber puts an apron on John.

The barber cuts John's hair.

John looks in the mirror.

The barber trims John's sideburns with a trimmer.

John stands up and brushes himself off.

John gives fifteen dollars to the barber.

UNIT 1 Check-in

Words and Phrases to Learn
- *luggage*: bags used when one travels
- *unattended*: alone; by itself
- *attach*: to put on; to connect to
- *boarding*: getting on

Key Expressions
1. Did you pack your own suitcase?
   = Did you pack the bags yourself?
2. ...points (sb) in the right direction = ...shows (sb) the way to go

Kim goes to the check-in counter.

Kim shows her mileage club card.

Kim puts her luggage on the scale.

The airline agent asks Kim about her luggage.

Kim gets a luggage ID tag.

Kim chooses a seat.

Kim receives her boarding pass.

The airline agent points Kim in the right direction.

Words and Phrases to Learn
- *empty*: to take everything out of
- *detector*: finder; sensor
- *head for*: to go toward
- *flight*: travel by airplane

Key Expressions
1. Please empty your pockets.
   = Take everything out of your pockets.
2. Step this way. = Walk here.

Kim puts her bag through the X-ray machine.

Kim puts her keys in the tray.

Kim walks through the metal detector.

The security guard picks up Kim's bag.

The security guard looks at Kim's pills.

Kim heads for immigration.

Kim gives her passport to the immigration officer.

The immigration officer stamps Kim's passport.

UNIT **3** Boarding

Words and Phrases to Learn
- *proceed*: to go
- *rows*: lines of seats
- *flight attendant*: (sb) working on a plane serving passengers
- *buckle*: to put on a belt

Key Expressions
1. I'd like to keep it with me.
   = I want to hold on to it.
2. Excuse me. = Pardon me.

Ladies and gentlemen, World Air Flight 225 to London is now ready for boarding. Please proceed to Gate 15 at this time.

Kim hurries to the gate.

We will now begin boarding rows 20 - 40.

Kim checks her boarding pass.

Here you are.

Boarding pass please.

Thank you.

Kim gives her boarding pass to the airline agent.

Where is seat 36J?

Just go straight and it's on the right.

Kim gets on the plane.

Would you like me to put up your bag?

No, thank you. I'd like to keep it with me.

overhead compartment

The flight attendant offers to help Kim.

Excuse me, sir. Could I get by? That's my seat by the window.

Kim moves to her seat.

No problem.

Thanks a lot.

The man stands up to let Kim by.

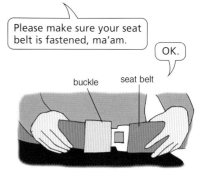

Please make sure your seat belt is fastened, ma'am.

OK.

buckle   seat belt

Kim buckles her seat belt.

Words and Phrases to Learn
- *passenger*: a rider; a traveler
- *discuss*: to talk about
- *announcement*: information given publicly or officially
- *turbulence*: rough air

Key Expressions
1. Please return to your seats. = Please go back and sit down.
2. Put your seat up. = Return your seat to its upright position.

Kim chats with the passenger next to her.

They discuss their travel plans.

The man puts his seat back.

The flight attendants serve drinks.

Kim pulls down her tray table.

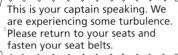

Kim hears the captain's announcement.

The man puts his seat back up.

Kim gets off the plane.

UNIT 5 Immigration (Arrival)

Words and Phrases to Learn
- *arrival*: getting (swh)
- *purpose*: reason
- *enter*: to put in; to type
- *claim*: to take as one's own

Key Expressions
1. Next, please!
   = Who is next in line?
2. Where will you be staying?
   = Which hotel will you be at?

Kim steps up to the immigration desk.

Kim hands her passport and card to the officer.

The officer scans the arrival card.

He looks at Kim's passport.

The officer continues to ask her questions.

The officer enters some information into the computer.

The officer stamps Kim's passport.

Kim takes back her passport.

Words and Phrases to Learn

- *realize*: to know suddenly
- *report*: to tell (sth) to an official person
- *describe*: to tell how (sth) looks
- *handle*: the part or piece on top to hold

Key Expressions

1 What should I do?
= Who should I speak with?
2 What does it look like?
= Can you describe it?

Excuse me. Where can I get my luggage?

What flight were you on, ma'am?

Flight 117.

Kim goes to the baggage claim area.

You can pick up your luggage at carousel 3.

Thank you.

carou

The airport attendant points to carousel 3.

Excuse me. My suitcase isn't here. What should I do?

You'll have to go to the baggage claim office.

Kim realizes her luggage is lost.

Can I help you?

Yes. My suitcase is missing.

ID tag

Kim reports her lost luggage.

Do you have your baggage ticket?

Yes, here it is.

Kim hands over her baggage claim ticket.

What does your suitcase look like?

It's small and blue with a silver handle.

Kim describes her suitcase.

Please fill out this form. Be sure you write your address.

Can I give you my hotel's address?

Yes, that's fine, ma'am.

form

LOST BAGGAGE

Kim fills out a form.

When your suitcase arrives, we'll deliver it to your hotel.

Thank you so much.

Kim gives the form back.

Words and Phrases to Learn

- *compact car*: a small car, usually with 2 doors
- *sedan*: a family car, usually has 4 doors
- *insurance*: a contract to pay money in case of a car accident
- *complete*: to fill in with information

Key Expressions

1 I'll need it for 5 days.
  = I'd like to take it for 5 days.
2 Have a nice trip. = Bon voyage.

Kim stands at the car rental desk.

The agent shows Kim the available vehicles.

Kim chooses a car.

Kim says how long she will need the car.

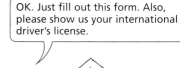

The agent gives Kim a form to complete.

The car rental agent suggests insurance.

Kim accepts a free map from the rental agent.

The car rental agent hands her the keys.

Words and Phrases to Learn
- *front desk*: the main counter at a hotel
- *check in*: to register and get the key
- *non-smoking room*: a room in which people can't smoke
- *hand over*: to give

Key Expressions
1. How will you pay for your room?
   = How will you be paying for that?
2. I'll use my credit card.
   = Can I put it on my card?

Kim enters the hotel.

The receptionist greets Kim at the front desk.

Kim puts her purse on the counter.

Kim tells the receptionist her name.

The receptionist checks the information on the computer.

Kim hands over her credit card.

Kim asks about her room.

Kim gets her room key.

UNIT 3 — A Telephone Call (from the Hotel)

Words and Phrases to Learn

- *wake-up call*: a phone call to wake (sb) up
- *ring*: to call by phone
- *local call*: a call to a number in the city; not long distance
- *check*: to make sure (sth) is correct

Key Expressions

1. Can I talk to...
   = Can you connect me with...
2. I'm calling about my bag.
   = I'd like to check on the status of my bag.

Kim rings the front desk.

The receptionist writes down the time.

Kim asks how to make a local call from her room.

The receptionist gives Kim instructions.

Kim dials the airport number.

Kim talks to the airline agent.

The man checks the luggage tag.

Kim thanks the man.

UNIT **4** The Hotel Concierge

Words and Phrases to Learn
- *concierge*: a hotel clerk who gives (sb) information or helps with problems
- *brochure*: a pamphlet
- *hours*: times (sth) is open for business
- *sightsee*: to visit and look around famous sites

Key Expressions
1. How long does it take to get there? = How far away is it by car?
2. My pleasure. = Glad to be of help.

Excuse me. I would like to visit Stonehenge today.

Alright. Here is a good brochure and map.

Kim gets some information from the concierge.

Pardon me. Are you from the States?

Yes, I'm from Austin.

A woman notices Kim's American accent.

I'm Ruth, from Atlanta.

I'm Kim. Are you going sightseeing today?

The women introduce themselves.

Yes. I'd like to see Stonehenge.

Ruth talks about her plans.

I have a car. Why don't we go together?

That'd be great. Thanks!

Kim offers to give Ruth a ride to Stonehenge.

1 How long does it take to get there?

It will take you about an hour and a half by car.

The concierge tells them how far away it is.

What are the hours?

It opens at 9:30 a.m. and closes at 6:00 p.m.

Kim wonders what hours Stonehenge is open.

Thanks for your help.

2 My pleasure. Enjoy your visit!

The women leave for Stonehenge.

UNIT 5 Sightseeing

Words and Phrases to Learn
- *arch*: a structure built around an opening
- *give back*: to return
- *background*: the scene behind (sb) in a picture
- *a bit*: a little

Key Expressions
1. What do you think?
   = How do you like it?
2. Let's get someone to take our picture. = Let's get our picture taken together.

> ¹What do you think?
> It's amazing!

Ruth and Kim walk around Stonehenge.

> ²Let's get someone to take our picture.
> Good idea!

Kim takes out her camera.

> Excuse me, sir. Could you take our picture for us?
> Sure.

turban

Kim asks a man to take their picture.

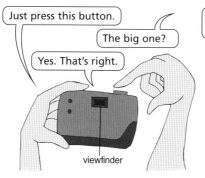

> Just press this button.
> The big one?
> Yes. That's right.

viewfinder

Kim shows the man how to use her camera.

> Can you get that arch in the background, please?
> No problem.

Kim tells the man what she wants in the picture.

> Can you move a bit to your left?
> Perfect.
> Is this OK?

The women change their positions.

> OK, Smile! One, two, three...

The man takes the picture.

> Thank you very much!
> You're welcome.

The man gives back the camera.

Words and Phrases to Learn
- *check out*: to pay a bill and leave
- *mini-bar*: a small refrigerator in a hotel room
- *charge*: the cost of (sth) on a bill
- *explain*: to tell the reason for

Key Expressions
1 I'd like to check out, please.
   = I'd like to settle up, please.
2 Please check your bill.
   = Could you please verify that the charges are correct?

Good morning, ma'am.

Good morning.[1] I'd like to check out, please.

Kim puts her suitcase down.

Of course. What is your room number, please?

617. Here's my key.

Kim returns her room key.

Thank you. Did you use anything from the mini-bar?

No, I didn't.

The receptionist prepares Kim's bill.

Alright.[2] Please check your bill and sign it.

The receptionist hands Kim the bill and a pen.

Excuse me, what is this charge here?

Kim points to a part of the bill.

That is for a call from your room.

Oh, yes. I called the airport.

The receptionist explains the charge.

Everything looks OK then.

Alright, here is your bill.

The receptionist gives Kim her bill.

Thank you for staying with us, Miss Jones. Have a nice day.

Thank you very much. Good-bye!

Kim picks up her bags and leaves.

Words and Phrases to Learn
- *glad*: happy; pleased
- *work out*: to exercise
- *pads*: (sth) to protect one's body
- *lock (sth) in*: to shut in and close with a key

Key Expressions
1 What sports do you like?
  = What kind of activities do you enjoy?
2 Are you ready? = All set?

Kim and Mary go to the park to exercise.

They take out their bags.

Kim puts on her rollerblades.

Mary sits down and takes off her shoes.

Mary puts on her pads.

They put their shoes in their bags.

They lock their bags in the car.

Kim and Mary put on their helmets and start to rollerblade.

UNIT 2 An Accident

Words and Phrases to Learn
- *balance*: feeling of one's weight being correctly held
- *kneel down*: to get on one's knees
- *sprain*: to hurt by twisting or turning too much
- *at all*: any

Key Expressions
1. Are you OK?
   = Did you hurt yourself?
2. What happened?
   = How did it happen?

Mary falls backwards.

Kim turns back to see Mary.

Kim kneels down beside Mary.

Kim checks on Mary.

Mary tries to move her wrist.

Kim helps Mary stand up.

Kim helps Mary skate back to the car.

Mary sits on the curb and gives Kim the car keys.

UNIT 3 — Making a Doctor's Appointment

Words and Phrases to Learn

- *swollen*: larger than normal
- *appointment*: a time to meet
- *as soon as possible*: at the earliest time
- *receptionist*: (sb) in an office who answers the phone

Key Expressions

1. I'd like to make an appointment.
   = I need to schedule an appointment.
2. Can you describe your problem?
   = What seems to be the problem?

Kim brings Mary some ice.

Kim suggests that Mary go to a doctor.

Kim passes Mary the phone.

Mary calls her doctor's office.

Mary asks to see the doctor as soon as possible.

Kim tells the receptionist her problem.

The receptionist looks at the schedule.

Kim hangs up the phone.

Words and Phrases to Learn
- *area*: place; space
- *direct*: to send; to tell to go (swh)
- *recognize*: to see and know; to understand from seeing
- *examination room*: a room where patients are seen by a doctor

Key Expressions
1. Why are you here?
   = What are you doing here?
2. The doctor will be with you soon.
   = The doctor will see you shortly.

Mary goes to the reception desk at the doctor's office.

Mary hands over her insurance card.

The receptionist directs Mary to the waiting area.

Mary recognizes someone in the waiting room.

Mary sits down next to Carlos.

The nurse calls the next patient.

Carlos follows the nurse to the examination room.

The nurse points to the examination room.

UNIT 5 The Examination

Words and Phrases to Learn

- *breathe*: to make air go in and out of the body
- *infection*: an illness caused by a virus or bacteria
- *fluids*: things like water or juice
- *prescription*: a note from a doctor listing the medicine a patient needs

Key Expressions

1 I see. = I understand.
2 Is it serious?
  = Is it a big problem?

Good afternoon, Carlos.

Hi, Dr. Graham.

They shake hands.

So, what's the trouble today?

Dr. Graham puts on some gloves.

I have a very bad cold. I cough all the time and my throat is very sore.

The doctor sits in front of Carlos.

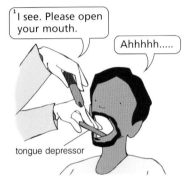

1 I see. Please open your mouth.

Ahhhhh.....

tongue depressor

Dr. Graham looks into Carlos's mouth.

Your throat is very red and swollen.

The doctor puts on his stethoscope.

OK. Now breathe deeply.

Carlos breathes deeply in and out.

Mmm... You have an infection. You need to take some medicine.

2 Is it serious?

Dr. Graham writes a prescription.

No. Just rest and drink plenty of fluids.

Thank you, Dr. Graham.

Carlos takes the prescription.

Words and Phrases to Learn

- *pharmacist*: (sb) trained to prepare and sell medicine
- *dosage*: how much medicine to take
- *side effects*: possibly bad things the body does because of medicine
- *soothe*: to cool or calm (sth) sore

Key Expressions

1 ...get a prescription filled
= ...receive the medicine listed on a prescription
2 You may have some dizziness.
= You might feel a little dizzy.

Carlos hands his prescription to the pharmacist.

Carlos waits for his prescription.

The pharmacist brings a bottle of pills to the counter.

Carlos asks about the dosage.

The pharmacist puts the bottle in a white paper bag.

The pharmacist gives Carlos the medicine.

Carlos asks about other medicine.

The pharmacist hands Carlos a pack of cough drops.

UNIT 1 Arriving at the Supermarket

Words and Phrases to Learn
- *groceries*: food and other necessities for the home
- *ATM*: a bank machine
- *shopping list*: a list of things that (sb) needs to buy
- *cart*: a big container on wheels

Key Expressions
[1] ...helping out = ...doing me this favor
[2] It's right here. = Here it is.

Peter and Julia arrive at the store.

Peter takes a cart from the aisle.

The shopping cart has a problem.

Julia chooses another cart.

Peter asks about the shopping list.

They look at the list together.

Julia takes money from the machine.

They begin shopping.

UNIT 2 Shopping

Words and Phrases to Learn

- *carton*: a box (with 12 places for eggs)
- *crack*: a small break
- *cereal*: (sth) like corn flakes which is eaten cold with milk
- *goods*: products

Key Expressions

1. Where can I find canned soups? = Where would the canned soups be?
2. Canned goods are in aisle 3. = Try aisle 3.

Julia picks up a carton of eggs.

Peter opens the carton and checks for cracks.

Peter puts the eggs in the cart.

They go and find the cereal.

Next, they look for soup.

Julia asks an employee about soup.

The employee tells her where to find the soup.

Peter picks up a can of soup.

UNIT 3 In the Baked Goods Section

Words and Phrases to Learn
- *baked goods*: things that can be bought in a bakery (e.g., bread, cakes, muffins)
- *rye*: a dark kind of grain
- *slice*: to thinly cut
- *loaf*: bread baked in one big piece

Key Expressions
1 Rye bread would be better.
= I would prefer rye bread.
2 Can you slice this, please?
= Could I get this sliced, please?

Julia and Peter come to the baked goods section.

Peter asks Julia about bread.

Peter suggests a loaf of rye bread.

Peter chooses a loaf.

Julia squeezes her loaf.

Peter asks the bakery worker to slice his bread.

The bakery worker slices the loaf.

She gives the sliced loaf back to Peter.

Words and Phrases to Learn

- *deli*: delicatessen; a place to buy cheeses, cold cooked meats and other snacks
- *cold cuts*: cold cooked meats and sausages
- *quantity*: amount
- *pepperoni*: a spicy sausage

Key Expressions

1. Can I have 250 grams of each, please? = Please give me 250 grams of each one.
2. You can pay at the checkout counter. = Please pay at checkout.

Peter and Julia arrive at the deli counter.

The deli employee arrives.

Julia orders cheese and meat.

The deli employee asks about the quantity.

Julia tells the deli employee how much she'd like.

The deli employee slices the meat and cheese.

He weighs the meat and cheese and puts prices on the bags.

He gives Julia the package.

UNIT **5** In the Produce Section

Words and Phrases to Learn
- *a half dozen* = 6
- *bin*: a big box or container
- *ripe*: ready to eat
- *feel*: to touch and check

Key Expressions
1 That's all I need.
  = I'm all done
2 That makes two pounds.
  = With this one, we're at 2 pounds.

What vegetables do you need?

I need some white onions.

Julia checks the list again.

How many do you need?

A half dozen.

Peter puts six white onions in a bag.

Anything else?

Peter puts the bag of onions in the cart.

1 That's all I need. How about you?

I want to get some fresh fruit.

They walk to the pear bin.

Are they ripe?

Yes. These are perfect!

Peter picks up some pears and feels them.

How much are these?

They're $2.35 a pound.

Peter puts the pears in the scale.

2 That makes two pounds.

scale

Julia adds one more pear to the scale.

I think that's all I need.

OK. Let's go to the checkout.

Julia puts the pears in a plastic bag.

Words and Phrases to Learn

- *item*: thing
- *checkout*: an area in a super-market where (sb) pays
- *express checkout*: checkout for people with few items
- *bagger*: an employee who puts groceries in bags at the checkout

Key Expressions

[1] Did you find everything you needed? = Did you get every-thing you required?

[2] Out of 45 dollars. = From 45 dollars received.

Peter and Julia arrive at the checkout area.

Peter suggests the express checkout.

The cashier greets them and they take out their groceries.

The cashier finishes scanning the groceries.

Julia gives the cashier the money.

The bagger asks what kind of bag they want.

The cashier gives Julia her change and receipt.

The bagger hands Peter the bag of groceries.

CHAPTER 11. SPECIAL OCCASIONS

UNIT 1 — Planning a Party

Words and Phrases to Learn

- *huh*: isn't that right; don't you agree
- *gather*: to collect; to put together
- *slip (sth) over*: to put (sth) on easily
- *agree*: to have the same idea or opinion

Key Expressions

1. Do you have plans next Friday?
   = Are you busy next Friday?
2. Is 6:00 OK with you?
   = How does 6:00 sound?

Mary and Julia talk after class.

They gather their books.

Mary slips her bag over her shoulder.

Julia puts her books in her bag.

They agree on the time.

They walk out of the classroom.

Julia offers to make a special dish.

Mary decides to make a cake.

Peter answers the telephone.

Peter leans against the kitchen counter.

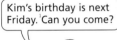

Mary tells Peter about the party.

Peter looks at his planner.

Mary checks Peter's name.

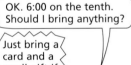

Peter says he will come.

Mary asks Peter for a telephone number.

Peter closes his planner.

UNIT 3 Other Plans

Words and Phrases to Learn
- *wallet*: (sth) in which to keep money, credit cards, etc.
- *coin*: small, round money made of metal
- *slot*: a small space to put things in
- *reach for*: to try to get with one's hand

Key Expressions
1. Don't worry about it.
   = It's no problem.
2. Don't mention it.
   = It's my pleasure.

John and Carlos meet by the vending machine.

Carlos takes money from his wallet.

He puts a coin into the slot.

Carlos pushes the button.

John reaches for the cans.

Carlos wants to pass along his congratulations.

John gives a can to Carlos.

They open their drinks.

UNIT 4 Party Preparation

Words and Phrases to Learn
- *banner*: a long sign
- *blow up*: to put air into
- *string*: a thin rope
- *decorate*: to put up/out special things for a party or holiday

Key Expressions
1. When is Kim coming?
   = When will Kim be here?
2. Can I help with anything?
   = Do you need me to do anything?

Julia shows her bag to Mary.

They walk to the dining room.

Mary opens the bag of balloons.

They blow up some balloons.

Julia ties some string to a balloon.

They decorate the dining room with the balloons.

John puts some snacks on the table.

John and Julia put up the banner.

UNIT 5 Wrapping a Gift

Words and Phrases to Learn
- *wrap*: to cover; to put paper/plastic around
- *fold*: to bend back as if to make two or more layers
- *bow*: a fancy ribbon
- *check (sth) out*: to go and see (sth)

Key Expressions
1 How much did it cost?
  = What was the price?
2 That's really cheap!
  = What a great deal!

What's next?

I still need to wrap Kim's gift!

Mary brings out some wrapping paper, scissors, and tape.

What did you get her?

I got her a vase for flowers.

Mary takes a vase out of a shopping bag.

That's nice! Where did you get it?

I bought it at The Home Arts Shop.

wrapping paper

Mary unrolls some wrapping paper.

¹How much did it cost if I may ask?

I got it for $25.

She cuts off a sheet of paper.

²That's really cheap!

Yeah. All their vases are on sale.

Mary places the box on the paper and folds up the sides.

When does the sale end?

tape dispenser

Julia tears off some tape and gives it to Mary.

Saturday, I think.

Mary folds the ends and tapes the paper.

Sounds great. I'll go check it out.

Yeah, you should. OK. We're done!

Mary places a bow on the box.

Words and Phrases to Learn
- *present*: a gift
- *light*: to start to burn
- *candle*: a small wax stick on top of a birthday cake
- *unwrap*: to uncover; to take the paper/plastic off

Key Expressions
1. I wouldn't miss it!
   = Of course I would come!
2. Who is this from?
   = Who gave this present?

Peter arrives at the party.

Mary takes the present from Peter.

Peter greets Kim and the others.

Mary brings in the birthday cake.

John lights the candles on the cake.

Kim blows out the candles.

Kim picks up a present.

Kim unwraps the present.

UNIT 1 Locations

Words and Phrases to Learn
- *men's wear*: clothes for men
- *employee*: a clerk; a worker
- *rack*: a storage shelf for thin square things, like CDs
- *album*: a set of songs released on one CD, record or tape

Key Expressions
1. Can you tell me where... = Do you know how I can get to...
2. Where can I find the blues CDs? = Do you know where the blues CDs are?

Julia and Carlos go into the Regent Mall.

The woman tells them where the store is.

Julia and Carlos ride up the escalator.

The Music Mart employee helps Carlos.

Carlos looks through the rack.

They try searching in a different place.

Carlos asks about the CD.

The worker points to another rack.

Peter tells the employee that he forgot his bag.

Peter describes his bag.

The woman writes down the details.

Peter shows the size of the bag with his hands.

Peter describes the material.

Peter lists the contents of the bag.

Peter leaves his contact information.

She offers to call Peter if the bag is found.

UNIT 3 A Cooking Lesson

Kim washes her hands in the kitchen sink.

Julia hands Kim a piece of cheese and a grater.

Kim grates the cheese while Julia washes the vegetables.

Julia puts the vegetables on a cutting board.

Julia puts a frying pan on the stove.

Julia takes a pan of chicken breasts out of the oven.

Julia slices the chicken breasts into strips.

Kim sprinkles some cheese on her fajita.

Words and Phrases to Learn
- *guy*: a man; a person
- *scrape*: to clear (sth) off from
- *rinse*: to clean with water
- *go out*: to go on a date

Key Expressions
1 He has a great sense of humor. = He is funny.
2 ...really hit it off = ...got along really well

Kim scrapes the plates into the garbage can.

They fill the sink with hot water.

Julia puts in some soap.

She puts on some rubber gloves...

...and washes a plate.

Kim takes the plate and rinses it.

Kim puts the plate into the dish rack.

Kim dries off a glass with a dishtowel.

UNIT 5 — A Movie Discussion

Words and Phrases to Learn
- *platform*: a landing, usually for (sb) waiting to get onto a train
- *special effects*: visual effects and action added to the movie
- *alright*: OK, but not great
- *thriller*: a kind of movie with a lot of suspense

Key Expressions
1. What did you think?
   = How did you like it?
2. He can play many roles.
   = He's very versatile.

John and Carlos walk down into the subway.

John buys two tickets.

Carlos puts his ticket into the slot.

They walk through the turnstiles.

John and Carlos wait on the platform.

They wait for the other passengers to get off.

They step onto the train.

They hold on as the subway begins to move.

Words and Phrases to Learn
- *countryside*: the scenery in the country, away from cities
- *awesome*: really great
- *photo album*: a book for storing photos
- *in person*: directly seen or done by (sb)

Key Expressions
1. It's much better in person. = It's much more impressive in person than in pictures.
2. What was the best part about your trip? = What did you like most on your trip?

I heard you went to England recently.

That's right. Would you like to see some pictures?

Mary and Kim walk into the living room.

Sure! How long were you there?

I was there for 10 days.

Kim takes out a photo album.

How was the weather?

It was sunny and cool. It only rained on one day.

Kim sits down next to Mary on the sofa.

It looks beautiful! Where did you stay?

In a lovely old hotel called the Plaza Hotel.

Mary looks through the album.

Wow! How was Stonehenge?

It was awesome! It's much better in person.

Kim comments on a photo.

Who's this?

Oh, that's Ruth. She's from Atlanta. I met her at the hotel.

Mary points to a person in a picture.

What was the best part of your trip?

I really loved the English countryside.

Mary asks about Kim's favorite part.

Thanks. Great pictures. Where would you like to go next?

I would like to go somewhere in Asia. Maybe Thailand!

drawers

Mary closes the album and hands it back to Kim.

Appendix

Clothing Size Conversion

Women's Clothing:

US	5	6/7	8/9	10/11	12/13
Europe	34	36	38	40	42

Women's Shoes:

US	4	5	6	7	8	9
Europe	35	37	38	39	40	42

Men's Shirts:

	small (s)	medium (m)	large (l)	extra large (xl)
US	34	36-38	40	42-44
Europe	87	91-97	102	107-112

Men's Shoes:

US	7	8	9	10	11	12
Europe	39	41	42	43	45	46

Metric Conversions

For Liquids:

To convert				
Pints	x	2	=	quarts
Quarts	x	0.5	=	pints
Quarts	x	0.95	=	liters
Liters	x	1.05	=	quarts
Gallons (US)	x	3.8	=	liters
Liters	x	0.3	=	gallons (US)

For Distances:

To convert				
Feet	x	0.3	=	meters
Meters	x	3.3	=	feet
Miles	x	1.6	=	kilometers
Kilometers	x	0.6	=	miles

For Weight:

To convert				
Ounces	x	28.4	=	grams
Grams	x	0.04	=	ounces
Pounds	x	0.5	=	kilograms
Kilograms	x	2.2	=	pounds

Common World Currencies

Country	Currency	Symbol
Australia	dollar (AUD)	$
Canada	dollar (CAD)	$
Europe	euro (EUR)	€
Japan	yen (JPY)	¥
Korea	won (KRW)	₩
Mexico	peso (MXN)	$
UK	pound (GBP)	£
US	dollar (USD)	$
China	yuan (CNY)	元
Taiwan	dollar (TWD)	圓

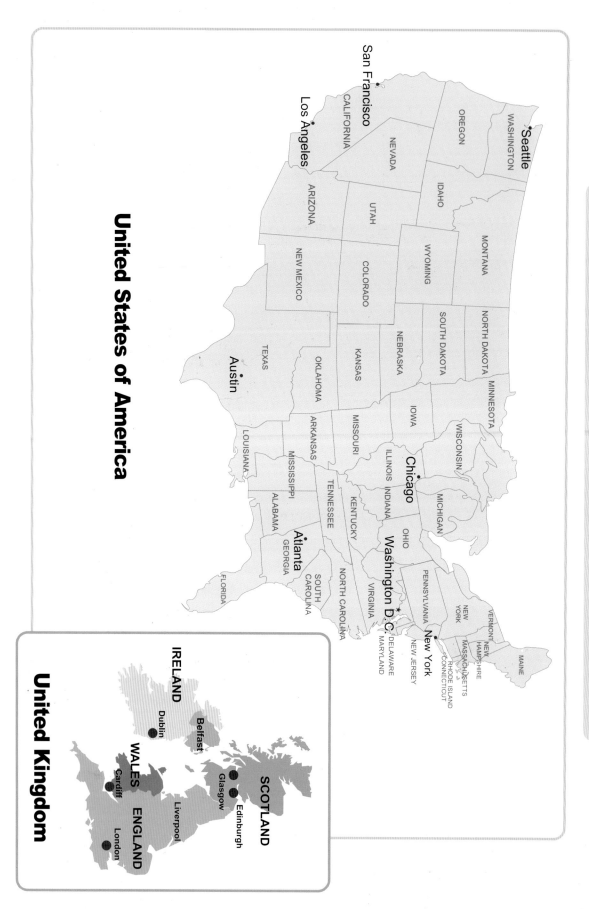

Maps for Reference

United States of America

United Kingdom